M W

G000153100

BUCKIN
RA ____S
Twelve Country Walks
around Buckinghamshire

Liz Roberts

With Historical Notes

COUNTRYSIDE BOOKS
NEWBURY, BERKSHIRE

First Published 1988
Reprinted 1989, 1991
© Liz Roberts 1988

COUNTRYSIDE BOOKS
3 Catherine Road
Newbury, Berkshire
ISBN 1 85306 004 6

Cover Photograph taken by Alan Charles
Sketch Maps by Bernard Roberts

roduced through MRM Associates Ltd, Reading
peset by Acorn Bookwork, Salisbury, Wilts
n England by J. W. Arrowsmith Ltd., Bristol

Contents

Sketch map showing locations of the walks.

Introduction

Buckinghamshire's very Englishness endears it to the rambler. Its landscape changes from peaceful pastureland and water meadows to hills and beechwoods, beautiful at all times of the year. The walks in this book have been chosen because they offer a good variety of the county's delightful scenery.

The gentle slopes of the southern Chilterns are heavily wooded, mainly with beech, giving the county its name of 'leafy Bucks'. Three small rivers, the Wye, the Chess and the Misbourne carve their way southwards to the river Thames which forms the county's southern boundary. These beechwoods end abruptly on the crest of the steep north-facing chalk slopes of the Chilterns. The scarp slopes drop away dramatically to the rich pastureland of the northern plain, broken by ranges of low hills fed by numerous streams. Across the hilltop runs the ancient Ridgeway or Upper Icknield Way. The Lower Icknield Way winds along in the valleys. It is a beautiful and historic route to travel.

All the walks are circular and their starting points have space for car parking. For those who like to break their walk for refreshment the names of good pubs and places serving tea along or near the routes are mentioned.

The historical notes are designed to provide basic information about the places of interest along the route, and will be found at the end of each chapter.

The sketch map that accompanies each walk is designed to guide walkers to the starting point and give a simple yet accurate idea of the route to be taken. The walks are all along public footpaths or permissive paths but do bear in mind that deviation orders may be made from time to time. For those who like the benefit of detailed maps the relevant Ordnance survey 1:50,0000 series will be useful. Please remember the Country Code and make sure gates are not left open or any farm animals disturbed.

No special equipment is needed to enjoy the countryside on foot, but do wear a stout pair of shoes and remember that at least one muddy patch is likely even on the sunniest day.

Many hours of enjoyment have gone into preparing these walks. I hope that the reader will go out and enjoy them too.

Liz Roberts   April 1991

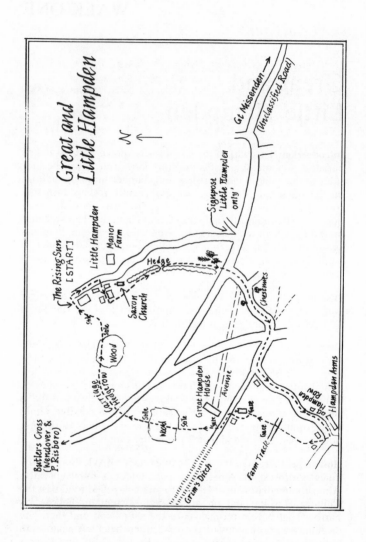

Great and
Little Hampden

Great and Little Hampden

Introduction: This part of the Chilterns is known as the walker's paradise; innumerable paths and tiny lanes run down the hillsides to the valley winding below and clamber up to the hilltops on the other side. Views of peaceful, gently rolling farmland, framed in the dark shades of the beechwoods, abound. Farmhouses nestle against the hills and Great Hampden House stands majestically high with a splendid avenue of trees, elm, lime and sycamore, leading up from the valley bottom. The hamlet of Little Hampden, a cluster of cottages, a farm, a pub and a tiny Saxon church, lies up the hill opposite.

Distance: 6½ or 5 miles – allow a good 3 to 4 hours for the longer walk as there is some quite steep climbing to do. O.S. Map Sheet 165 Aylesbury and Leighton Buzzard.

Refreshments: There are pubs at Little Hampden, where the walk starts, and at the halfway mark at Hampden Row. The genial host of the *Rising Sun* at Little Hampden becomes less genial at the mere sight of muddy boots or shoes so these must be removed before entering. The walk has been so arranged that a stop at the *Hampden Arms* for a drink or lunch is possible, either inside or in the pleasant garden at the side of the pub. Both these houses open 12 noon and at 7 pm in the evening.

How to get there: On the A413 Amersham to Aylesbury road 6 miles northwest of Amersham, pass under a railway bridge. Almost immediately bear left on to an unclassified road past the Chiltern Hospital and on into Great Missenden. Follow the narrow High Street through until the shops end and there are dwellings on both sides of the road, then bear left again onto another unclassified road signposted Butlers Cross and Princes

7

Risborough. After two miles take the second of two narrow lanes on the right signposted 'Little Hampden only' and wind carefully uphill through high hedges occasionally giving way to wide sweeping views over the hillsides. About a mile up the lane on the left is the little church and, on the right, Manor Farm. At the end of the lane is the *Rising Sun*. There is a small area for parking on the right or, just past the pub, the track runs into woodland where it is possible to park.

The Walk: Retrace the route past the front of the pub and on down the lane to a track on the right by an attractive brick cottage and walk past two white farm cottages and the farm on the left. Turn left down a path at the next cottage on the right and follow the path along the back of the farm and the hedge on the left. There are beautiful views all round as the path descends; Courtfield House, a large white building, can be seen across the fields. There is a rather indistinct gap in the hedge through which the path passes; look out for a curved arrow 'footpath' sign painted on a telegraph pole. Turn right through the hedge and, keeping it now on the right side, follow the path on down the hill. Blossoms of scabious and wild roses deck the hedgerow in summer. At a brake of conifers this rather tatty path bears right again and follows an overgrown route between the woodland on the left and the hedge on the right and emerges finally on to the road at a Public Footpath sign opposite a lane leading to Great Hampden.

Cross the road and follow the lane winding steeply uphill to Great Hampden. Shortly, on the right, appears an avenue of huge trees, elms, limes and sycamore mostly, said to have been planted in honour of a visit by Queen Elizabeth I to Hampden House, which can now be seen on the right. The broad avenue leads down to the road in the valley and, at its entrance, are two small lodges known as the Pepper Boxes because of their unusual shape.

At the road intersection continue sharply right under the branches of three overhanging Spanish chestnut trees and continue uphill along the leafy lane, bearing sharply right again where two public footpaths emerge onto the road on the left. At the crossroads, keep straight on. Facing straight ahead is the metalled drive to Hampden House with a triangle of grass at the roadside by the lodge. Here bear sharply left and follow the winding lane which meanders from left to right to Hampden Row – a row of cottages on the left and the *Hampden Arms*, also on the left at a crossroads.

At the *Hampden Arms* cross the road and take the track opposite between delightful cottages buried in flower-filled gardens. Soon the track emerges into an open field. Keep to the path, along a ridge, across the field and cross the metalled farm track to a gate on the far side. Go through the gate and follow the obvious track across a large grass field close to the newly erected fence. Clumps of elms provide grateful shade for the grazing cattle. Pass through another gate ahead and follow the path to the gate into Great Hampden churchyard and enter through it.

Take the path to the left through the churchyard leaving the church on the right and turn left onto the drive of Great Hampden House. On the left is the splendidly tall Tudor stable block and, on the right, the house itself here more or less hidden from view by trees. Very shortly the house comes into view behind a majestic carriage sweep in the centre of which is a huge ancient Cedar tree. Its companion was blown down in gales a few years ago completely crushing the small car parked beneath it. Just past the house go through the white gate ahead onto a grass track and immediately over a stile on the right into a grass field. Here there is an excellent view of the long south front of the 15th century battlemented house. It has recently been extensively restored, stucco removed and the old warm brick revealed. After the Second World War it became a boarding school for girls and remained so until recently when it was sold to be used now as a film studio.

Follow the field path across the front of the house to a stile on the far side entering woodland. Cross the stile and follow the path through a plantation of conifers on the left and mixed woodland on the right. The path descends gently to two stiles which are crossed to enter a large cultivated field. Cross this field diagonally; the path is always clearly re-instated by the farmer after ploughing so is well-defined but can be muddy. Across the valley to the right can be seen the warm red brick of the timber-framed farmhouse. The path emerges onto the road over a stile.

Cross the road to the gate opposite with a Public Footpath sign against it and go onto the track, Carriage Hedgerow, leading up through the beechwoods, decked with bluebells in the spring.

9

After about ⅓ mile take a small path to the right (watch out for the white arrow footpath sign to indicate this painted on a tree) and go through the wood edge to another stile to another well-defined path across a cultivated field. Pause here to look back over the valley at the splendid patchwork of fields, plantations and mixed woods on the far side. At the top of the field the path creeps through the hedge to a stile. Over the stile is a small area of conifers and scrub and the path leads to another stile. Go over the stile and follow the path diagonally across a cultivated field. The field is littered with large flints and, in winter is cold and exposed on the hillside and can be muddy. Cross the track at the top of the field and follow a signposted grass path opposite between an orchard on the left and a white cottage and garden on the right. The path emerges on to the lane above the *Rising Sun* where the car is parked.

The walk can be reduced by 1½ miles if, instead of bearing left at the triangle of grass by the lodge of Hampden House the walker proceeds straight ahead up the drive with the tiny parish church of St Mary Magdalen on the left and the house on the right to the white gate on the far side of the house. Go through this and carry on as for the longer walk. Hampden Row and the Hampden Arms are missed out.

Historical Notes:

Great Hampden House, as it stands today, is a heavily Gothicised 18th century house but it has been the site of the Manor house since the 11th century and the home of successive Hampdens, Earls of Buckingham. Set in a high downland park, surrounded by beechwoods and arable fields, the house commands a majestic view of the valley which divides the two Hampdens. It was at one time the home of John Hampden, cousin of Oliver Cromwell. He is famous for his refusal to pay the notorious 'ship-money' imposed by Charles I. It is said that he rode his horse one Sunday morning down through the beechwoods and up the hill to Kimble church where he rode into the church during Morning Prayer and disrupted the service to rally his tenants and neighbours to follow his example. He died of wounds sustained at Chalgrove Field in 1643 and was buried in the churchyard opposite the house. The tower in the centre of the long south front of the house is said to be of 14th century origin. The last Earl of Buckingham to live in the house was a much-loved and respected 'Squire' known to all the villagers and who knew them by name also. A great cricket enthusiast, he organised in 1950 the laying down of a cricket pitch which lies beyond the *Hampden Arms* and is kept immaculately.

Little Hampden Village: The 15th century two-storey timber-framed porch of the church gives it the look of a picturesque farmhouse. Manor Farm is on the other side of the lane and a delightful hotch-potch of roof shapes is made by its collection of weather-boarded barns. Banks of purple willow-herb encroach on to the grassy lane edge where the woodland is halted. At the top of the lane, which is a dead end, lies the Rising Sun pub. Until recently a small country pub frequented by locals and walkers, it has been cleverly extended, the extension being a mirror-image of the original and the clientele has now also been 'extended' to embrace young business men and the 'smart' set.

Church of St Mary Magdalen, Great Hampden: The church of St Mary Magdalen is of flint with some stone facing and has a clerestoried 13th century nave. Unfortunately the church is kept locked as a precaution against vandalism. It houses an intriguing monument to John Hampden, who died in 1643 after wounds sustained at Chalgrove Field during the Civil War. The monument, designed for his grandson by Henry Cheere in 1743, is of two cherubs, one of whom appears to be waving a funny hat on a stick, seated on a sarcophagus surmounted by a large oval medallion depicting the Battle of Chalgrove Field.

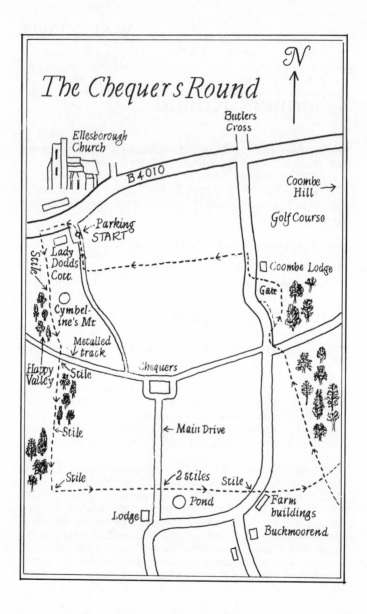

Chequers Round

Introduction: This is a moderately strenuous walk, up and down hill, through some of the loveliest Chiltern countryside and past Chequers, the country retreat of British Prime Ministers since it was given to the nation in 1917 for this purpose by Lord Lee of Fareham. Small sections of the ancient Ridgeway are travelled too.

Distance: A circular walk of 4 miles which should take about 2 hours. O.S. Map Sheet 165 Aylesbury and Leighton Buzzard.

Refreshments: There are no cafes along the route but there could be no more ideal place to picnic on a fine day than on the humped shoulder of Cymbeline's Mount overlooking the multi-coloured woodland of Happy Valley.

How to get there: Take the A40 toward Oxford out of High Wycombe and, at the Pedestal roundabout at West Wycombe, turn right on to A4010 Aylesbury road. Above the roundabout stands the mausoleum of the Dashwood family. About three miles past Princes Risborough, just beyond an inn on the left, The Bernard Arms, bear right onto B4010 Kimble to Wendover road and, in about a mile, park the car opposite Ellesborough church in a small lane marked with a Public Footpath sign.

The Walk: The walk starts on the other side of the two charming almshouses next to the car, known as 'Lady Dodd's Cottages'. The church of St Peter & St Paul opposite, rises on a steep hillock from the flat vale and three neat thatched cottages snuggle under its benign shadow. Cross the stile on the far side of the almshouse gardens and cross the field upward along a chalky track. At the hedge at the top of the field cross another stile into a grass field where cattle are often grazing. On the left is Cymbeline's Mount or Castle, a seven-metre high mound. This is

13

of Iron Age origin and an Iron Age fort is hidden in the scrub on the right.

Follow the well-defined path round the humped shoulder of the mount with the land dropping abruptly away on the right toward Happy Valley. The deeply grooved dry valley, a characteristic of chalky Chiltern upland, meanders downhill through countless shades of green, yellow, russet and crimson massed together in the many varieties of trees. Cross the stile at the end of the grass field and enter the wooded valley, downhill and then uphill on a stepped path. On hot summer days the dizzy scent of boxwood is almost overpowering here. After crossing the next stile, pause to take in the magnificent view of the broad, saucer-like Vale with its blue-hazed ridge of low hills on the horizon. On the extreme left the sharp edge of hills descends near Wainhill and, on a clear day, the white cooling towers of Didcot power station can be seen beyond. Cross the cultivated field and keep to the path through a small copse and cross the metalled drive to the 'back door' of Chequers. Cross the stile on the other side of the drive and follow the path along the edge of the wood. In spring this beechwood is carpeted in bluebells, a cerulean sea beneath the sharp acid-green of the young beech leaves trailing almost to the ground. In late summer and autumn one may stumble upon a dozen pheasants feeding in the field.

After crossing the stile at the end of the wood, Chequers appears on the left in a shallow dip. The path, part of the Ridgeway, originally ran across the front of the house but, for security reasons, it was decided to close this section. Local ramblers and conservationists strongly opposed the closure so the path was eventually re-routed some $\frac{1}{4}$ mile from the front of the house. The glass building to be seen at the front was once an orangery but Mr Edward Heath, when Prime Minister, had it converted into a swimming pool. Towering above and behind the house is Coombe Hill, the highest point of the Chilterns at 876 feet. On top of it stands a stone monument, a gold painted pineapple decorating its top, commemorating those who died in the Boer War. Some twelve years ago the monument was struck and riven by lightning. Stone quarried in Cornwall was brought by sea from Newlyn to London whence it was brought by road to repair the monument and a sturdier lightning conductor was fitted. Across the fields can be seen the mellow shapes of

Buckmoorend Farm and its buildings with a lovely backdrop of woodland against which they seem to huddle.

Having followed the path parallel with Chequers for $\frac{1}{4}$ mile alongside a wood and over a stile, the path (waymarked Ridgeway) turns abruptly left over a cultivated field which can be very muddy. Cross two stiles at the far end of the field then the main driveway to Chequers, from where an excellent view of the house may be had, and a stile on the far side of the drive into a large grass field. Follow the obvious path across the field, skirting a dewpond and a clump of trees on the right, to a stile on the far side emerging on to a minor road. There are bends on both sides here, so cross with caution, and enter the wooded track opposite with farm buildings on the right.

Follow the track (Ridgeway) for about $\frac{1}{4}$ mile climbing gently to a crossway. Here turn left away from the Ridgeway and follow the bridlepath through the woodland where, in late summer, the purply-pink of willowherb forms great splashes of colour, onto a minor road. Turn left on to it and then right onto the road opposite the arched gateway leading to the back of Chequers, and after a few yards take a track on the right leading back into woodland. Follow this track, ignoring the fork on the left, until a small wooden gate is reached. Go through the gate and another one down on the left and carry on down the track between Ellesborough Golf Course and farm cottages to the road. Turn right and cross the road; in about 100 yards take the signposted footpath on the left, a broad band of grey-white chalk snaking across the huge field uphill to a fine view of Ellesborough church at the top. Turn right at the field exit and follow the track downhill for $\frac{1}{4}$ mile to the almshouses and the parked car.

Historical Notes:

Chequers: The house is well-known today as the country home of Britain's Prime Ministers for the house was presented to the nation by its owner, Lord Lee of Fareham, for this purpose in 1917. Built on the site of an older house by William Hawtrey in 1565, Chequers has been much renovated, firstly in the Strawberry Hill Gothic style of the late 18th century, then again in the 19th and restored to almost its original style in the 20th century by Sir Reginald Blomfield. On the first floor, the Great Parlour still contains its pilastered panelling and there are Cromwell family portraits in the Long Gallery. The second floor still contains the 'prison room' where Lady Jane Grey was confined for two years. Prime Ministers are not permitted to leave any personal items at Chequers and, in the time of Stanley Baldwin, this posed quite a problem as he was always leaving his beloved pipes behind at the house.

Ellesborough Church: The flint church of SS Peter and Paul, has an embattled tower in mixed Perpendicular and Decorated styles much restored by the Victorians between 1854 and 1871. The Hawtreys of Chequers are commemorated in brass on the church wall. The benign ghost of the Reverend Robert Wallis, rector of the Parish of Ellesborough before the Civil War still haunts the church and was reputedly seen by the current incumbent on the path quite recently.

Cymbelines Mount: This was the stronghold of the British King Cunabelin from whom two local villages, Little and Great Kimble, derive their names. Relics indicate that there was a Romano-British village, a Roman villa and a Neolithic hill camp in the vicinity.

Waddesdon

Introduction: Waddesdon village, on the main Aylesbury to Banbury road, is influenced and dominated by the Manor, built between 1874 and 1889 by Baron Ferdinand de Rothschild in French chateau style and perched on top of Lodge Hill. Its turrets obtrude from among dense woodland to bring a breath of Touraine to an otherwise very English landscape. The park, through which the walk goes, has been planted with a great variety of trees and is farmed on its outskirts. The countryside is beautiful; gently undulating hills with splended views of the Vale of Aylesbury from their tops.

Distance: 5½ miles – an easy 2½ hours' walk taken, for the most part, on grassy verges of metalled drives and across farmland. O.S. Sheet 165 Aylesbury & Leighton Buzzard.

Refreshments: There are four pubs in Waddesdon all offering bar meals. The Five Arrows is nearest to the start of the walk.

How to get there: From Aylesbury take the A41 Bicester/ Banbury road and Waddesdon is reached in 6 miles. The main road curves sharply to the right and then straightens up into a wide High Street. There is parking by the shops on the right but, to avoid crossing this busy thoroughfare, take a small left turn, Baker Street, between the red brick village hall and the Five Arrows Hotel and park the car a short distance up there.

The Walk: On leaving the car go on down Baker Street until it curves sharply left and take the footpath opposite the corner on the right. Turn left at the end of the short path onto a drive and follow it for 100 yards. Then turn left at a junction opposite the cricket pavilion on the right.

Follow this drive for a mile, keeping straight ahead where tracks cross, through gentle parkland on the left and, to the right,

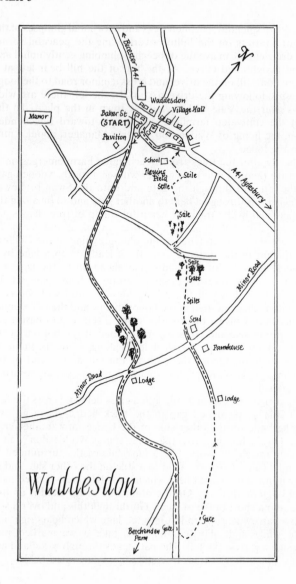

a wealth of splendid specimen trees and occasional glimpses of the Manor's turrets on the hilltop overlooking the peaceful scene. The drive enters an avenue of beeches climbing gently uphill and round a righthand curve. At the top of the hill bear left at a Y-junction, still on the drive, and cross a minor road to the lodge opposite, following the drive past it. To the left there are wide views over the Vale with Aylesbury town in the plain. To the right the cultivated farmland rises gently toward Beechenden Farm, the home of Waddesdon's Estate Manager, about a mile from the lodge.

Shortly after the track from Beechenden Farm emerges on to the drive (about ⅓ mile) the walker will see a sturdy wooden gate on the left. Go through the gate and onto the Swan bridleway following this through a field to another gate and so on along the well-defined bridle track. A beautiful clump of tree shapes can be seen on the hilltop to the left, varied in colour and depth. To the right the view stretches to the blue-grey line of the Chiltern escarpment in the distance. The track leads on to a lane by a lodge at the edge of the estate. Go ahead on to the lane and follow it uphill toward a dramatic group of Scots pines at the top and then downhill toward Waddesdon Stud with views of Quainton village nestled in the hollow below and the tall, slender chimneys of Calvert brickworks in the distance. Go past a red brick farmhouse and cross the minor road at the bottom of the hill to a footpath opposite which leads along beside the immaculate stud farm. Ignore the path to the left at the end of the buildings and follow the waymarked path – a yellow arrow indicates it.

Bear right to go over a stile into a grass field and cross the field to a stile in an arched gap in the thick hedge. Then go over another stile on the other side of the hedge into another grass field. On the hilltop across the valley stands Waddesdon Manor, looking for all the world like a fairy-tale castle, surrounded by splendid trees. Cross the field to a stile on the other side and go over it into a cultivated field which cross by a well-defined path, kept open at all times. On the other side of the field is an iron gate into a short brake of trees. Go through this and over a stile into a narrow lane. Turn left into the lane which bears right in a little while and, shortly after this, take a waymarked path through a gap on the left. The path leads through woodland and a new plantation of trees to a stile into a cultivated field.

Follow the path across the field keeping the rugby posts to be seen in the school playing field slightly to the right to a stile in the hedge. Over the stile turn right and follow the path between a fence and the boundary of the school field. The path used to run straight across but the thriving school has taken over more field for games so the path has been re-aligned to go round it. Turn left at the corner of the playing field and follow the same path all the way along, past the gardens of some houses, to the school entrance. Turn right away from the entrance and left at the end of School Lane and so back into Baker Street, bearing right at the bend to go back to the parked car.

Historical Notes

Waddesdon Estate: The estate of Waddesdon was bought by the Baron Ferdinand de Rothschild in 1874 from the Duke of Marlborough and work was begun at once on the preparation for the manor on Lodge Hill. The top of the hill was flattened, a steam tramway built from the railway at Quainton and a team of Percheron mares was brought from Normandy to haul the yellow Bath stone for the building on the top while fully-grown trees of exotic types were imported to plant round it. The house, in the style of a French Renaissance chateau, was designed by the French architect, Gabriel-Hippolyte Destailleur and the gardens were laid out by a French landscape gardener, Laine.

The house, which was presented to the National Trust in 1957, holds a unique collection of Sevres china, exceptional 18th century English portraits and paintings of many earlier Dutch and Flemish masters as well as many fine examples of French 18th century furniture.

The house is open to the public from March 25th to October 25th and admission for non-National Trust members is £2.50. It is closed on Mondays and Tuesdays. There is a tea-room in the Old Kitchen and Servants' Hall.

The church of St Michael: This church is of 12th century origin with additions in the 13th and 14th centuries and a 15th century clerestory. The ornate alabaster pulpit came from the Great Exhibition of 1851 and was given to the church by the Duke of Marlborough.

The Claydons

Introduction: A pleasant, not too strenuous walk through three small villages of black and white cottages built through the centuries to house rural craftsmen and estate workers. Now many of them have been knocked together to make larger houses. The walk traverses peaceful pastureland with fine open views and passes alongside the west front of Claydon House, the home of the Verney family.

Distance: 8 miles which can be covered in 3 to $3\frac{1}{2}$ hours. O.S. Map Sheet 165 Aylesbury & Leighton Buzzard.

Refreshments: There are a number of pubs in Winslow which serve bar meals and snacks, and tea may be had at Claydon House. It is a National Trust property open to the public from May to October every day except Monday and Tuesday. It is not necessary to go into the house for tea which is served in the stable block to the right of the house.

How to get there: Take the A413 Aylesbury to Buckingham road to Winslow where follow the minor road straight ahead signposted 'The Claydons'. After a mile take a small road on the right also signposted Claydons and follow this winding lane for $2\frac{1}{2}$ miles into East Claydon. On entering the village, just before the crossroads, turn sharp left into a No Through road and almost immediately right into a cul-de-sac by the church where you can park your car.

The Walk: Take the footpath alongside the old vicarage; in about $\frac{1}{4}$ mile it emerges onto a minor road and, bearing left, runs parallel with it into the village of Botolph Claydon. Though East Claydon possesses the church, Botolph Claydon in the same parish, was always the larger settlement. A clock tower on the

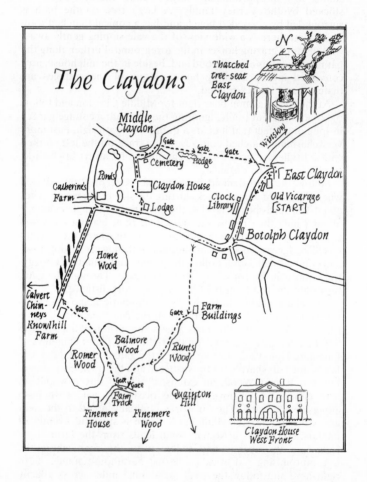

The Claydons

Thatched tree-seat East Claydon

Middle Claydon

Gate

Gate Gate

Cemetery Hedge

Winslow

Ponds

Catherine's Farm

Claydon House

East Claydon

Clock Library

Old Vicarage [START]

Lodge

Botolph Claydon

Home Wood

Calvert Chimneys Knowlhill Farm

Gate

Gate Farm Buildings

Balmore Wood

Runts Wood

Romer Wood

Golf Gate

Farm Track

Finemere House

Finemere Wood

Quainton Hill

Claydon House West Front

other side of the road, built in 1913, separates the two, having one clock face for each community. Next to the clock tower stands a disproportionately large Public Library built and stocked by the Verney family. A large tree on the path is surrounded by a wooden bench and has a conical thatched roof. To the left there is a wide view of the vale sloping gently away, with fields of grazing horses in the foreground. Further along the path on the left is a small pond and, beside it, the mill house, now converted into a dwelling house. Many of the cottages are thatched and timber-framed.

At the road junction bear right for Middle Claydon and follow the road for about $\frac{1}{4}$ mile, ignoring the stile into a cottage garden in spite of the fact that it bears a Public Footpath sign. Past more very charming thatched cottages take a track on the left marked with a bridleway sign. The tall chimneys of Calvert brickworks can be seen in the distance.

Follow the well-defined track to the edge of Runt's Wood where turn right along a track skirting the side of the wood. After about 100 yards bear left on to the grass track through a gate for about $\frac{3}{4}$ mile then follow the track half right leaving the wood edge and passing through tall grass and bracken, the ancient mixed hedgerow speckled in summer with flowers of dog rose, and enter a small copse. Follow the grassy, and sometimes boggy, track through the copse to a rusty iron gate. Through the gate, turn right on to a farm track for a very short distance.

Ahead and slightly to the left is the dramatic shape of Quainton Hill, erupting like a bubble from the flat plain and below is Finemere Wood. In 200 yards, past some farm buildings on the left, take the gate to a track on the right. The Tudor chimneys of Finemere House may just be seen as the gate is closed. Here the landscape falls sharply south-westward and the track leads downhill into Romer Wood, an extensive area of mixed woodland with clumps of foxglove and the occasional wild rose bush alongside the track. Then it works gradually uphill to the neat and comfortable Knowlhill Farm. Here a splendid avenue of poplars, straight as a Roman road, leads from the farm. Turn right into the avenue and follow it to the road where the uncompromising red-brick Catherine Farmhouse stands. Turn right here and follow the road for about $\frac{1}{2}$ mile, across a lazily flowing brook, Claydon Brook.

Enter Claydon Park by the lodge on the left and follow the

bridlepath, bearing left, past the house on the right. To the left runs the brook which broadens out into three crescent-shaped lakes to the west of the house fashioned in the late 18th century to look as if they had existed since the beginning of time. Clumps of elms, planted at the same time, have fallen victim to the Dutch Elm disease which was particularly virulent in Bucks a few years ago. Often the banks of the stream and lakes are lined with fishermen patiently watching immobile lines.

Past the house go through a kissing-gate on the right and turn left on to the main drive. Look back for a view of the front of the house which is well worth a visit if time (and footwear) permit. If not strike off down the drive, avoiding the sheep who munch and dawdle their way about the grass verges. Turn right again onto the road at the end of the drive and walk up through Middle Claydon, a straggle of cottages and a huge old vicarage. The church of Middle Claydon, All Saint's, stands on a hillock only a few yards from Claydon House, literally in the garden.

Follow the road past a small cemetery on the right ignoring the stile in the far corner and, in a few yards, turn right again through a green metal gate into a farm track. The track soon peters out but the path continues along the field edge with the hedge on the right. At the corner of the field, where the hedge ends, the path strikes straight across a cultivated field to two gates lying between two dead trees set starkly against the skyline. The farmer does not always reinstate this path but there is a public right of way across the field used by the people of the village, so forge ahead. On the other side take the left hand gate alongside another field and through a gate to a grass field where cattle are grazed. Go through the gate on the far side of this field and emerge on to the village road, where turn right again and follow the road across the crossroads and ahead to the No Through road, the cul-de-sac and the parked car. On sunny Sundays an ice-cream man sometimes parks here and is a welcome sight.

Historical Notes:

Claydon House and grounds: Claydon House is the home of the Verney family. Out of the pleasant lush countryside a park was formed to the west of Claydon House between 1763 and 1776. Clumps of elms were planted, three crescent-shaped lakes made and shrubs and plants were imported from Belgium. Though it was at first intended that Capability Brown should be commissioned to landscape the park, it was in fact fashioned by James Sanderson of Caversham whose charges for the lay-out amounted to £3,339. Sanderson may have been responsible for persuading his employer, the 2nd Earl Verney, to remove the churchyard which lay at that time between the house and All Saints, Middle Claydon. The villagers viewed this action with horror and felt it was bound to bring misfortune down on the Verney family. The church, on its hillock, is now in the middle of the garden of Claydon House. Inside it there is a bust of Sir Edmund Verney, killed at Edgehill in 1642 and a monument designed for his son, Sir Ralph Verney, by an Italian artist.

Though there have been Verneys in Buckinghamshire since the 13th century, Edmund Verney was the first of the family to reside at Claydon having purchased the lease from one Martin Lister in 1620.

The Civil War rent the Verney family into two opposite camps. Sir Edmund died fighting for his King at Edgehill and his eldest son, Ralph favoured the Parliamentarians while the youngest son, Mun, was taken prisoner fighting for the King at Drogheda and murdered. However the family fortunes were revived with the Restoration. Sir Ralph's estates were restored to him and he was made baronet.

In 1956 the Verney family gave Claydon House, with part of the garden and parkland, to the National Trust. Mr and Mrs Ralph Verney now live in the Victorianised south wing. Summer evening concerts are frequently held in the house, often for some charitable purpose.

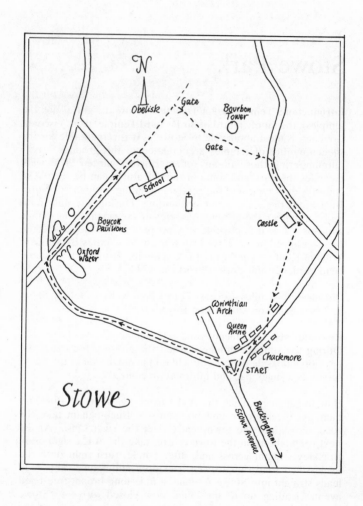

Stowe

Stowe Park

Introduction: Templa quam Dilecta – 'How delightful are the temples', the family motto of Sir Richard Temple, later Viscount Cobham, is most applicable to Stowe as it is remarkable for the sheer quantity of temples accumulated in the grounds, vastly outnumbering those of any other English garden. The walk encircles the park and some of these features can be seen. The countryside is typical of the gently undulating farmland of North Bucks and the walk is not demanding. During late July until mid-September the grounds themselves are open to the public and, for a fee, it is possible to view part of the house and the park, designed in the early 18th century by Charles Bridgeman, William Kent and, later on, by 'Capability' Brown who became head gardener and clerk of works in 1741.

Distance: 5½–6 miles – an easy 2½ to 3 hour walk. O.S. Map Sheet 152 Northampton and Milton Keynes.

Refreshments: The Queen Anne at Chackmore serves bar meals. During the summer holidays, when the grounds are open, the pavilion alongside the cricket field on the north side of the house serves as a snack bar and information centre.

How to get there: Take the A413 from Aylesbury to Buckingham. At the major roundabout outside Buckingham take the road across into the town centre over the river Ouse. At the next roundabout, in the town centre, take the A422 signposted Brackley straight across and, after ¼ mile, turn right onto the unclassified road signposted Chackmore and Stowe. This road leads straight into Stowe Avenue, a mile-long broad, tree-lined avenue leading up to the main, now closed, drive to Stowe through the Corinthian Gate. At the end of the avenue, on the right, is the little village of Chackmore. Turn first right and immediately on the left is a convenient small lay-by for parking the car.

The Walk: On leaving the car return to the avenue and turn left across the main drive to take the minor road signposted Stowe. Walk along this country road for one mile with views of rolling farmland on the left and glimpses of the park on the right.

After a mile turn right at the crossroads and enter Stowe by the Oxford Lodge over the Oxford Bridge traversing a rather sluggish bit of water. Go straight on up the handsome drive bordered by lime trees and on past the Boycott Pavilions, one on each side and now the homes of members of the school staff. Soon the green roof and colonnades of the school chapel may be seen among buildings on the right.

At a sharp right bend in the drive keep straight ahead on a path running along the far side of the school cricket field. The obelisk to be seen across the fields to the left is a monument erected in 1759 to commemorate the heroic death of General Wolfe whose storming of the Heights of Abraham secured Canada for the British Commonwealth. Soon, on the right, the magnificently colonnaded north front of the school can be seen across the cricket field, an equestrian statue of George I in front of the entrance.

After ¾ mile turn right through a gate on to a wide grass track and follow it ahead to a gravel path. Cross the path and take the gate on the opposite side into a grass field toward a rather plain monument to the Duke of Buckingham and Chandos in the middle. To the right can be seen the tiny church of Stowe where 'Capability' Brown was married and which is now the sole remaining building of the village of Stowe, and the Cobham monument from whose tower parts of five counties may be seen. It was designed by James Gibbs in 1747. The bogus folly, Stowe Castle, can now be seen ahead on the horizon. Keep on across the field to the far corner with the Bourbon Tower about 80 yards to the left. Go through an iron gate and walk eastward down the field edge to a narrow road where turn right toward Stowe Castle, which has now been converted into a handsome dwelling house.

After ½ mile, passing the castle entrance on the right, look out for a waymarked footpath to Chackmore on the right. The path is a little difficult to see but go over the iron gate and proceed straight across the field ahead southward to a gap in the hedge opposite. Go through the gap over a low strand of barbed wire and cross the next, cultivated, field to another gap in the hedge in the far corner. Go through this gap into a grass field and cross to a rickety gate near a red brick house. Go over the gate and turn right into the road back to Chackmore. Bear left past Manor Farm to find the car.

If the walker finds grappling with barbed wire and scrambling through hedges daunting, it is perfectly simple to continue up the road past Stowe Castle to a T-junction where turn right into the road back to Chackmore.

Historical Notes

Stowe: The original house of Stowe was built in the late 17th century, a handsome, not overly large, gentleman's home. By the early 18th century it was the seat of Sir Richard Temple, later Viscount Cobham, who set about massive improvements. He engaged Charles Bridgeman, a brilliant landscape designer, to work on the gardens. By introducing a ha-ha, or sunken fence, Bridgeman did away with any enclosing fence or wall and threw the gardens open to the countryside.

Viscount Cobham's nephew, Earl Temple, succeeded to the property on Cobham's death and set about transforming the house to be worthy of its fabulous gardens. To the North front he added the beautiful colonnades and Robert Adam designed a magnificent new South front, both completed in the 1770s.

At the end of the First World War there was an acute shortage of vacancies at major public schools. Fortuitously, Stowe was put up for sale by Baroness Kinloss, daughter of the 3rd Duke of Buckingham and Chandos, and the house and gardens were sold to a Mr Shaw who made it available for a new public school 'to rank, if possible, among the first six'. Stowe School was born on May 11th, 1923.

Grand Avenue: Approaching Stowe along the Grand Avenue off the Brackley road, one passes a pair of Georgian lodges on one of which is a circular plaque commemorating the purchase of the avenue by Eton College in 1924. It was donated to the new school by the old and this generous act on Eton's part probably saved it from the maws of some speculative builder. The Corinthian Arch was designed by Thomas Pitt in 1765. Through it the South front of the house can be seen.

The Oxford Lodge: This was designed by Kent for a different site and was re-erected at the entrance to Stowe with the addition of pavilions in 1760. The road ahead is Roman. The Oxford Bridge was built in 1761, a charming piece of foolery with its ornate urns and rustic stonework.

The Boycott Pavilions: These were designed by Gibbs in 1728 but were altered by Giambattista Borra in 1758. Borra was employed by Lord Temple to modify many of the garden buildings which he did skilfully and tastefully.

The Bourbon Tower: Once a keeper's cottage, it was renamed to commemorate a visit of the exiled French royal family in 1808.

WALK SIX

Olney and Emberton

Introduction: The walk starts in Olney, follows a footpath through Emberton Country Park and into farmland along a bridlepath to the hamlet of Filgrave and then back over the fields to the peaceful little village of Emberton and so by another path back through the country park to Olney. The park was the inspiration of the local District Council: the council converted the hideously scarred countryside, the result of quarrying gravel for the building of the M1 motorway, into a series of lakes and recreation areas. The scheme won them a Countryside Award. Now grown in, with reedy banks to the lakes and well-planted trees, it would be difficult to imagine it as ever having been anything else.

Distance: 6 miles – a comfortable 2½ hour walk with no steep ups or downs. O.S. Map Sheet 152 Northampton & Milton Keynes.

Refreshments: Olney abounds in offers of hospitality and food with three pubs all serving bar meals and innumerable small cafes and restaurants. Also, on the edge of the town, is a wine bar offering good food and wine. The Cowper and Newton Museum offers tea when it is open – on Tuesdays and Saturdays from 10-12 am and 2-5 pm. There is also a pub in Emberton, about ¾ of the way round the walk.

How to get there: From Junction 14 of the M1 Motorway follow the A509 toward Newport Pagnell and then as it swings right at a roundabout signposted for Wellingborough. Olney is seven miles from the M1 junction on the A509. There is car parking in the Market Square in the town centre on the right but it is limited. However, at the far end of the broad High Street there is ample parking which is not limited by time or space.

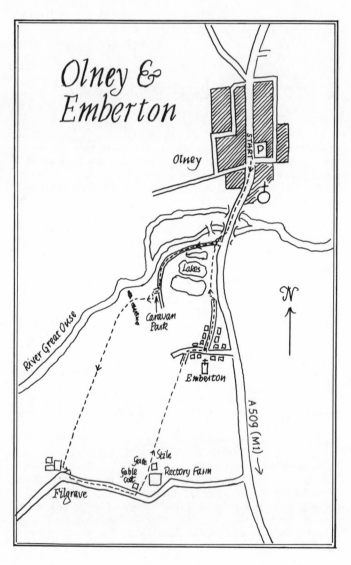

The Walk: Turn left out of the car park and walk south through Olney, passing a lovely mix of 17th and 18th century domestic architecture, over the two bridges spanning the river Great Ouse and the weir. After the second bridge take a path on the right across a grassy space with a third, flood, bridge on the left and turn right on to the metalled track. Follow this pleasant track through the Country Park with lakes on which there are sailing boats and children canoeing. Many varieties of water bird are on the left and the quietly flowing Ouse on the right.

After about one mile, at a broad sweep to the left of the track around the lake end, there is a small permanent caravan park on the right. Go into the caravan park and turn left then, almost at once, turn right between two caravans at a large wooden box-like affair marked 'HOSE REEL' in red paint and behind the caravan on the left is a rickety five-barred gate. Go through the gate and follow the marked footpath across a cultivated field to a gap in the opposite hedge. Go through the gap onto a bridle track and, keeping the hedge on the right, follow this track over fields for some 1½ miles. On either side are expansive views of the rich farmland; dark chocolate coloured soil and fields of sheep and sleek Jersey cattle. To the right can be seen the village of Weston Underwood, on the horizon the spire of Stoke Goldington church stands out.

Filgrave, a handful of houses around the farm, is entered at Manor Farm, huge and prosperous-looking. Just before the farmyard itself turn left on to a concrete track toward a Public Footpath sign 30 yards ahead. Go through the footpath gate and on to the road where you turn left. About ½ mile up the road, just past Gable Cottage on the left, take the rickety stile in the hedge on the left (waymarked) and walk north-eastward toward Rectory Farm to a gate in the far left corner of the field just past a rather plain, square cream-coloured house, out of keeping with the warm red brick of the farmhouse and its buildings.

Follow a new 'Bridleway' arrow along the hedge to a stile. Go over the stile and walk across a cultivated field, aiming slightly to the right of the squat tower of Emberton church ahead, and go through a gap in the hedge just to the right of a clump of tall trees forming part of the hedge. Cross the bridleway just before the gap and then go straight on into the field following a marked footpath across it to another gap on the far side and thence on to a grass track leading into West Lane Farm. From West Lane

Farm turn right into West Lane and walk on past the church on the right to the clock tower in the village centre. At the tower turn left into Olney road and follow this pleasant quiet road, once part of the main road to Wellingborough, past charming houses and pretty gardens and then, at its end, where the signs for Emberton Country Park appear, turn left into it and take the path on the right beside the Toll-Booth (pedestrians don't have to pay). Follow the path back to Olney crossing the grass by the flood bridge and up the little gravel path back on to the bridge over the weir. The spire of Olney church is visible for most of the walk back, acting as an excellent landmark.

Historical Notes

Olney: The town has very much a feel of Northamptonshire about it being right at the northern tip of Bucks and certainly the church looks much more a product of that county unlike its stout, embattlemented neighbours deeper into Bucks. Were it not for the constant traffic through its busy High Street, the charming little town of Olney, dominated by its pale, tall, slender church spire, could have turned its back on the 20th century. Great care has been taken to ensure that no inappropriate shop facia offends blatantly and the many little 'courts', which are entered through ancient cobbled alleys often supported on huge 17th century oak beams, are clearly marked without fussiness. Each is an individual delight.

The town is set in a gentle bowl of hills on a bend of the river Great Ouse and was the home of the poet William Cowper and John Newton who was curate-in-charge from 1764-1780 and a former slave-trader. Together these two produced the 'Olney Hymns' of which the most well-known are *Amazing Grace*, *Glorious things of thee are spoken* and *O, for a closer walk with God*. Their museum stands on the right of the market square and holds an excellent diary of Newton's life, in particular during his slave-trading days. Olney is most famous nowadays for the Pancake Race which takes place from its High Street on Shrove Tuesday. A small plaque on the wall of the delicatessen shop states: 'Pancakes start here'.

Church of SS Peter & Paul: This church is large with a west tower and spire nearly sixty metres high, one of only two Medieval towers in the county. The church is of 14th century origin but much renovated and 'repaired' in the 18th, 19th and 20th centuries.

Mill House: Beyond the churchyard, in a peaceful riverside meadow, lies the 18th century Mill-house, all that now remains of a once thriving mill.

Church of All Saints, Emberton: This stands on a little hillock in the village whose centre is defined by its clock tower of creamy ashlar stone, with pinnacles and large lancets, which was built as a memorial to the second wife of the Rector, Thomas Fry, in 1846 and named 'Margaret's Tower'. Memorials of both World Wars decorate another side of it. The tower replaced a great elm tree surrounded by a stone wall, the site being known as Emberton Cross.

Emberton Country Park: This park covers an area of 70 hectares in the Ouse valley, transformed from the floodland and disused gravel pits into a park with a wildlife reserve, areas for camping and boating and a wetland nature reserve.

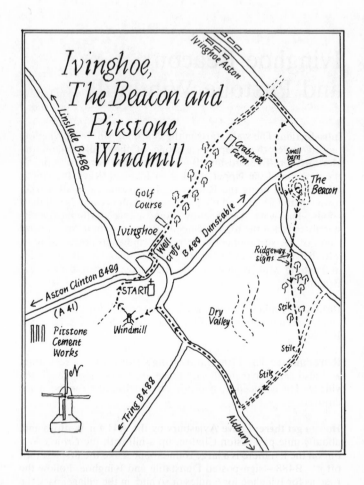

Ivinghoe,
The Beacon and
Pitstone
Windmill

Ivinghoe Aston

Linslade B488

Crabtree
Farm

Small
barn

The
Beacon

Golf
Course

B 480 Dunstable →

Ivinghoe

Well-
croft

Ridgeway
signs

Aston Clinton B489

↑ START

(A 41)

Dry
Valley

Stile

Windmill

Pitstone
Cement
Works

Stile

N

Stile

Tring B488

Aldbury →

Ivinghoe Beacon and Pitstone Windmill

Introduction: The walk starts in the charming village of Ivinghoe tucked under the steep scarp slope of the Chilterns on the Hertfordshire/Bedfordshire/Buckinghamshire borders. It lies at the junction of the Upper and Lower Icknield Ways, the Upper Icknield Way being the Ridgeway. It was once a small market town where farmers and the local straw plaiters came to sell their goods. The walk starts gently along a level path but climbs steeply to reach the top of Ivinghoe Beacon, with its spectacular views of the surrounding countryside, and then descends again into the valley by way of the Ridgeway path and across the fields to Pitstone Mill, reputed to be the oldest post-mill in Great Britain.

Distance: $7\frac{1}{2}$ miles. Allow a good $3\frac{1}{2}$ to 4 hours for the walk; the climbing is quite strenuous. O.S. Map 165 Aylesbury & Leighton Buzzard.

Refreshments: The 17th century *King's Hotel* offers a restaurant and also serves bar meals and there are two other pubs in the village. On a fine day, a picnic on the Beacon can be much enjoyed.

How to get there: Leave Aylesbury by the A41 for Watford and, about $\frac{3}{4}$ mile past Aston Clinton, up a hill with the *Crow's Nest Inn* on the left there is a large roundabout. Take the first left turn off it – B488 – sign-posted Dunstable and Ivinghoe. Follow the road as for Ivinghoe for 6 miles or so and, in the village, park the car neatly between the wall of the church and the handsome bus shelter.

The Walk: Turn right and walk westward along the side of the churchyard. Notice opposite a charming house with two portraits of Queen Victoria in the stucco dated, on the left 1837, and on the right 1897. The old Rectory, a 16th century timber-framed building refaced in 18th century brick in delightful Strawberry Hill Gothic style, is passed and then a lane – Vicarage Lane – leads off to the left. A group of pretty cottages lies on the right. Follow the lane to *The Rose & Crown* pub where turn right into Wellcroft, alongside some modern houses towards the Golf Club. Soon the lane ends at the Golf Club and becomes a field path through pleasant tree-broken farmland. Follow the path, which is well-used, through woodland climbing steeply on the right and giving way every so often on the left to wide views of cultivated fields and meadows. There is a splendid brake of giant beech trees on the left just before the path emerges finally into open countryside again and the hamlet of Ivinghoe Aston comes into sight ahead and to the left. The actor Bernard Miles lived at Ivinghoe Aston and the broad accent he adopted is very typical of the country people of this Hertfordshire/Buckinghamshire border. Soon the pink-walled buildings of Crabtree Farm come into view on the right and, to the left a handsome stables and horses grazing in the nearby field.

The path joins the lane past the entrance to Crabtree Farm and at its end turn right and follow the road gently uphill for about ⅓ mile and, on the second bend, look out for a Public Footpath sign well concealed in the hedge on the right. Take this footpath, achieved by climbing a rusty iron gate, and forge ahead due south diagonally across two large cultivated fields. The farmer does not always re-instate the path after ploughing so it is not easy to see, but there is a public right of way across both fields which emerges on to the busy B489 Dunstable road at another Public Footpath sign close to the hedge in the far righthand corner of the second field.

On the opposite side of the road is a lane leading up to Ivinghoe Beacon. Cross the road with caution and enter the lane. Almost immediately a path, with Public Footpath sign, leads off to the left and climbs steeply up to the Beacon. However, it is often overgrown and nettley so, if preferred, the walker can continue winding up the lane until, at a righthand bend with a sign directing to the car park on the opposite side and a two-way Ridgeway sign on the bank, turn left on to a well-defined track and follow it up, down and up again on to the top of the Beacon. The views from here are quite awesome all round. To the west and north the villages of Ivinghoe and Ivinghoe Aston can be seen. Southwest, the belching chimneys and modern buildings of the Tunnel Cement works at Pitstone dominate the scene, eastward the hills roll on toward the steep slopes on which Whipsnade Zoo stands and, to the south, are the wooded coombes and rises of the typical Chiltern landscape. Glimpsed between the trees, the wide sweep of water of Wilstone Reservoir may be seen gleaming.

From the top of the Beacon, take the broad track downhill to the lane, which can be seen, and cross it to the bank with the Ridgeway signpost. Follow the track to the right indicated by a stone Ridgeway sign near the ground. Go over a stile shortly and follow the path across a grass field slightly uphill to where a Ridgeway sign – an orange acorn – can be seen on a post at the wood edge. Enter the scrubby woodland and follow the path through to another stile onto a broad track running both ways and turn right on to the track. To the right the downland falls steeply away into a dry valley typical of the chalky terrain. The path runs down hill round the valley and crosses another stile. Clumps of mullein and foxglove clothe the side of the track and orchids may be found in the grassland. Occasionally clumps of wild raspberries, small and pippy fruits, may be found at the wayside. Now the cement works will be in view dead ahead. The waymarked track crosses directly over two fields, over stiles, on to a narrow lane. Turn right and follow the lane downhill for about ½ mile to the B488 road. Turn right again and walk down the road toward Ivinghoe. At a sharp right-hand bend in the road with a lay-by on the left there is a gate and stile leading on to a path to Pitstone windmill. Cross the stile and follow the path to the post-mill, the oldest in the British Isles having been built in 1624. From the mill, turn right and follow a path across a cultivated field to a well-defined track where turn right again. Cross the field by the track and re-enter Ivinghoe village through a gap between charming 16th and 17th century houses. At the end of the path turn right again and walk up the village street to the church and the parked car.

Historical Notes:

Church of St Mary the Virgin, Ivinghoe: The church is 13th-14th century; much restored in 1871 by G. E. Street. The tower is 14th century but its copper spire is of later date. The roof is supported by comic and grotesque corbels and angels with outstretched wings. There is an original Jacobean pulpit and some large poppy-head pew-ends. On the church wall are two ancient artefacts; a thatch-hook which was used to drag thatch off a burning building to save further damage and a man-trap, a truly fearsome implement used, until the middle of the last century, by landowners and set to discourage the entry of poachers or other intruders on to their land.

Pitstone windmill: The oldest surviving post-mill dates from 1624. It was extensively repaired by volunteers in 1963 using the timbers of the original mill, dated 1627 and 1749. It is a National Trust property and is open to the public on Sunday afternoons and Bank Holiday Mondays from 2.30 pm to 6 pm from May until September. There is a small museum inside the mill.

Chalfont St Giles and Jordans

Introduction: The first mile of this walk, starting just beyond Milton's cottage in the village of Chalfont St Giles, is along a busy though unclassified road with a good footpath alongside a great variety of houses dating from Victorian and early 20th century to modern housing estates. The village itself surrounds a small green with a pond and, behind it, the Norman church and it is bounded by the river Misbourne. The walk continues across fields skirting Seer Green and enters Jordans by the 'back door'. Through the village of Jordans the walk continues across more fields to return to Chalfont St Giles.

Distance: 5½–6 miles – a comfortable walk with only short steep stretches which should take about 2½–3 hours, depending upon how long the walker chooses to spend admiring the warm red-brick exterior or the equally warm wooden interior of the Friend's Meeting House at Jordans. O.S. Map Sheet 176 West London.

Refreshments: There are three or four inns in Chalfont St Giles all providing bar food and there is *Milton House* restaurant opposite Milton's cottage. There are, however, no facilities for refreshment en route though excellent wooden benches surround Jordans village green for the would-be picnicker.

How to get there: Chalfont St Giles is approximately three miles south-east of Amersham. Take the A413 from Amersham and, at a mini-roundabout opposite an imposing Public House called *The Pheasant,* turn right into the village. Follow the road through the village for about ½ mile; Milton's cottage is signposted outside and lies on the left opposite the Milton House restaurant. Just

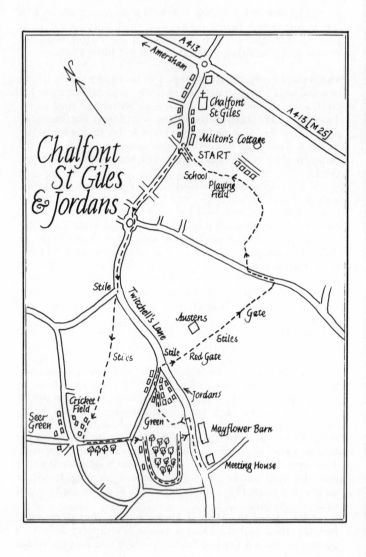

a little further uphill on the left is Hillside Close where it is convenient to park the car off the busy road. There is a free car park on the right just into the village if the walker wishes to browse round and then walk up the hill to Milton's cottage.

The Walk: Leaving the car walk back to the road and turn left on to it and walk along, straight across a mini-roundabout at the hill crest, for one mile. At the Y junction, where the road meets Twitchell's Lane and New Barn Lane, where there is a triangle of grass, cross the road and go over a stile on to a waymarked footpath. Follow the footpath straight across two fields and over two more stiles until a cricket field is reached on the edge of Seer Green.

Still keeping straight ahead with the high hedge on the left walk across the cricket field and take the tiny path in the far corner. Follow this path with a wire fence on the left and a hedge on the right. In 20 yards turn right on the path at the field edge between pretty cottage gardens and the yard of Manor Farm. At the end of the path turn left onto a shady track with a narrow strip of woodland on the right and open views of pasture land on the left, marred only by the pylons striding across the countryside. Proceed downhill and then uphill, crossing a narrow track in the valley bottom, past some elegant houses into Jordans.

Turn right onto a narrow road at the top of the incline and follow this round for about ⅓ mile shaded by the lovely beechwood on the left, a legacy to Jordans given by the 1st Baron Trent of Nottingham and Henry Cadbury and permanently reserved as an open space since 1934. In the corner, where the walker bears up to the left, a memorial stone and a seat can be seen. In about 100 yards there is an entrance to a path on the right through a gate; all the information about the path is on a notice facing the other way. Go through the gate and across the field to a lane where the Mayflower Barn can be seen opposite. Turn right onto the lane, which is busier than it seems, and walk ¼ mile downhill to the Friends of Jordans Meeting House, a mellow red brick 17th century house set in an orchard-fringed valley on the left.

Having visited the Meeting House retrace your steps uphill past the Barn and the Quaker Guest House next door to a turning on the left marked Public Footpath and Jordans village only. Take this turning into the quiet and peaceful village. Cross the green diagonally to the impressive Village Stores and Post Office opposite and turn right onto the road. Follow the road directly between pleasant houses with shrubby gardens until it ends at the gates of Jordans First School. Here take a small path on the left alongside the school and follow it downhill to a track. Turn right onto the track and follow it, bearing left at its junction, to emerge onto the lane again.

Almost exactly opposite, on the right side of the lane and next to a house called Twitchell's End, is a well-concealed Public Footpath sign. Cross the stile here and go up through a shady pathway to a red painted iron gate. Go through the gate and follow the well-defined footpath ahead through small grass fields and over three more stiles. On the left can be seen the warm red brick and timbered Austen's farmhouse. Continue as straight as possible along the defined path, through large untidy fields, over two more stiles, through a kissing gate and a large gap in the hedge to emerge on to a road. Turn left onto the road on the other side of which is a convenient metalled path and walk along it for ¼ mile to a waymarked path on the right just before the 30 mph limit sign.

Follow the track, bearing right at the fork, past a small strip of woodland and then turn left at a Public Footpath sign across a smoothly mown grass field. Keeping to the edge, with the hedge on the right, go through a gap at the edge of the wooden fence ahead and carry straight on past a small housing estate on the right and over some playing fields to arrive at a wire fence. Take the metalled path in the right-hand corner against the fence and follow this ahead and downhill past the school to the road again. Turn left to find the parked car in Hillside Close.

Historical Notes:

Chalfont St Giles: The village is best known for its association with the poet, Milton, though he never actually owned the cottage which bears his name. When the Great Plague hit London in 1665 Milton besought his friend, Thomas Ellwood, to find a refuge for him and his family in the country. Milton only lived in the cottage for about a year but it was here that he completed his work, *Paradise Lost* and began on its sequel,

Paradise Regained. The cottage, purchased by public subscription in 1887 in honour of Queen Victoria's Jubilee, is now a museum.

St Giles' Church: The Norman church of St Giles has a Perpendicular west tower but much external restoration was carried out in Victorian Decorated by G. E. Street in 1863. The chancel, nave and aisles are all 13th century and the wall paintings are of 14th and 15th century origin.

Jordans is 'Quaker' country, the land for the village having been purchased by the Society of Friends in 1915. Here a village – designed to surround a green – was to be built where artisans and others could apply their skills for the benefit of the community. Unfortunately, the communal project, Jordans Village Industries, failed but the charming cottages built to house the workers still surround the village green. There is an air of serenity and peace about this quietly unhurried place.

Old Jordans Farm, where Quakers used to meet in secret before the Toleration Act of 1688, has been purchased by the Society of Friends and is now in use as a Guest House and Conference centre. Next door is the Mayflower Barn built, it is said, out of timbers from the *Mayflower* which bore the Pilgrim Fathers to America.

The Quaker Meeting House, built in 1688 by the widow of Isaac Pennington of Chalfont St Giles, is of simple red brick with a hipped roof covering the one-storey room. Inside there is a low balustraded platform for the elders and a timbered gallery. The house is open to the public on every day except Tuesdays from 10 am to 1 pm and from 2 pm to 6 pm or dusk in winter. In the grounds are simple headstones commemorating William Penn, two of his wives and sixteen of his children; also Thomas Ellwood, Milton's friend and tutor to the Pennington family.

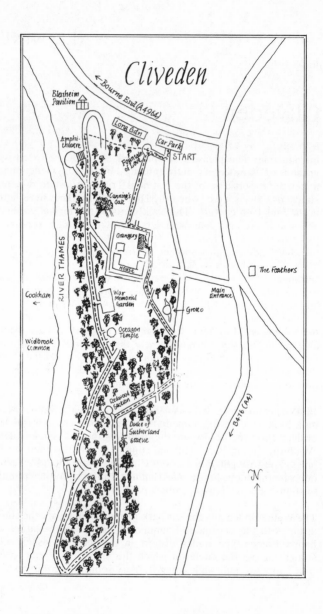

Cliveden

Introduction: The pleasure of this walk through the extensive grounds of Cliveden is greatly enhanced by the knowledge that, under the expert care of the National Trust, the estate remains almost exactly as it was when the Duke of Sutherland lived here in the mid 19th century. The walk starts in the formal gardens near the house and then meanders downhill through tree-lined paths to the river Thames, along it for about a mile or so and then back up through woodland to the house itself.

Distance: $4\frac{1}{2}$–5 miles. Most paths are gravelled and all are well-defined and the walk will take about 2–$2\frac{1}{2}$ hours at a leisurely pace. O.S. Map Sheet 175 Windsor & Reading.

Refreshments: Morning coffee, light lunches and teas are available in the Orangery restaurant near the car park from April to October from Wednesdays to Sundays each week and there are designated areas for picnicking in the grounds. *The Feathers*, opposite the entrance gate serves bar meals.

How to get there: Take the A4 from Slough towards Maidenhead and, in about 5 miles, immediately after going under a railway bridge, take the B476 on the right signposted Taplow and Wooburn. Go up Berry Hill and continue along this road for $3\frac{1}{2}$ miles. The wrought-iron gates of Cliveden lie on the left exactly opposite the public house, *The Feathers*. Entrance to the grounds for non-National Trust members is £1.50.

The Walk: On leaving the car park turn right and walk the short distance to the enormous Fountain of Love, where statues of happy French-type nudes disport in a huge cockleshell. Go straight across the circle on which this stands to a wide grass 'ride' opposite and walk along it. Very soon a path bisects the

47

ride and, to the right, is the formal Long Garden with magnificent examples of topiary. The walker is free to divert and stroll in the garden. At the end of the grass ride is a gravel path and a stretch of open grassland. The Blenheim Pavilion, built in 1727 to commemorate Lord Orkney's command of a brigade at the Battle of Blenheim, stands rather forlornly among the trees on the right. Walk across the grass in front to a grass path leading downhill to the small Amphitheatre where turn left at the wooden fence.

After about 300 yards an enormous oak tree, its outstretched boughs supported by massive tree trunks, is approached. This is Canning's Oak, so-called because the statesman is said to have spent hours sitting in its shade to admire the distant view down the river. At the oak bear right onto another gravel path toward the War Memorial Garden which is reached down a few steps on the left. Conceived as an Italian Garden, during the First World War it was adapted as a cemetery for those who died in the military hospital on the estate. Having viewed the garden, return to the gravel path and on to another set of steps, up this time, to the Octagon Temple, converted to a chapel in 1893. Turn right across the front of the temple and follow the path through yew trees and box to the river below. The heavy scent of the box leaves on a hot summer's day is all-pervading.

At the river bank turn left along the path past the boathouse and follow this riverside walk, between the trees banked on the cliff-like escarpment on the left and the serene river on the right, for a little over a mile passing an estate cottage on the right. At a point where the path appears to divert from beside the river, turn round to see the house, majestically dominating the view over this lovely stretch of the Thames. Then take a path (hairpin) to the left which winds steeply uphill through the woods to the Grand Walk, a broad track running parallel with the river above the steep gorge. The trees are mixed and very colourful, especially in the autumn; there are many fine tall beeches among them. To the left are glimpses of the river, the wide expanse of Widbrook Moor and the hills around Cookham Dean on the Berkshire bank. A blue haze seems to hang between the trees above the water as it makes its quiet way through the deep, chalky gorge. After about a mile the track turns right at a corner where stands a statue of the Duke of Sutherland surveying the house he built from across the splendid formal parterre. Down the steps to the left is an enormous sequoia tree-section, part of a giant redwood brought to Cliveden from California by Lord Astor.

Follow the path past the Duke's statue across one cross-path and, in 20 yards, to another cross where turn left down a broad grass 'ride' between tall beeches to a smaller path on the left going downhill to the Flint Grotto. Past the grotto follow the path downhill, across a metalled driveway on the valley floor and down and up a stepped path opposite continuing up the steps as the path turns right toward the corner of the house. Turn right through the yew hedge at the corner and right again through a wrought-iron gate past the Orangery restaurant. Go through the yew hedge at the far end and turn right down the drive back to the Fountain of Love and turn right again to return to the car park. The famous water garden lies a short distance to the left of the car park and is well worth a visit, as is the Rose Garden.

Historical Notes:

Cliveden: The present mansion at Cliveden stands on the site of two earlier houses, both destroyed by fire. The first house was built on the flattened hilltop for the 2nd Duke of Buckingham between 1677 and 1679 by a Dutch architect, Winde. The Duke had a grand terrace made in front of the house and the parterre which was levelled by piling up earth to form the terrace. At the time there must have been marvellous views over the surrounding countryside but subsequent growth of trees has now restricted the view. Lord Orkney, the first British Field Marshal, bought the estate in 1696 and employed Thomas Archer to add colonnades and wings to the house. He also employed a landscape gardener by the name of Henry Wise to improve the gardens. This house was destroyed by fire in 1795 and William Burn's classical new house was completed in 1829 but, again, destroyed by fire in 1849. The new owner, the Duke of Sutherland, employed Sir Charles Barry to build a new house and, in 1893, it was purchased by the American William Waldorf, later Lord Astor.

During the 1930s the house was the centre for the 'Cliveden Set' so named by Claude Cockburn to describe the Astor family and their friends who thought peaceful negotiation could be achieved with Adolf Hitler, but, in fact, Lord Astor's son and his daughter-in-law, Nancy, made it a centre for both the literary and political society of the day.

During the Second World War, the Canadian Red Cross Memorial Hospital was built in the Cliveden estate and, at the end of the war, was given by the Canadians to the National Health Service where it served the local community until 1984.

The Astor family lived in the house until 1966 though the estate had been given to the National Trust in 1942.

The Thames at Dorney and Boveney

Introduction: A gentle walk through the water meadows and along the Thames bank through Dorney village to Boveney Lock and back across Dorney Common. The name Dorney is a derivation from the Saxon 'Island of Bees' and the village has, since Domesday, been famous for its honey. The manor was mentioned in the Domesday Book. The right to graze cattle on Dorney Common goes back to feudal times and there are still cattle grazing on the unenclosed pasture. Cattle grids now surround the common but, earlier in the century, it was gated.

The walk can be combined with a visit to Dorney Court, a 16th century manor house situated in the village. The river Thames forms the southernmost tip of the county boundary here.

Distance: 5 miles. There are no hills to climb so the walk will take about 2½ to 3 hours. O.S. Map Sheet 175 Reading & Windsor.

Refreshments: There are two inns in the village both of which serve bar food and tea may be had at Dorney Court which is open to the public from 2 pm to 5.30 pm on Sunday, Monday and Tuesday and Bank holidays from Good Friday until October. Alternatively, nothing could be more pleasant than a riverside picnic on a sunny day.

How to get there: On the A4 from Slough westward, turn left at a small roundabout signposted Dorney – B3026, Lake End road – and follow the road through Dorney village to park the car on the common on the far side. There is a convenient piece of flat ground on the right by the entrance to Pigeon House Farm.

The Walk: Retrace the route back through Dorney village passing some fine examples of timber-framed buildings, both large

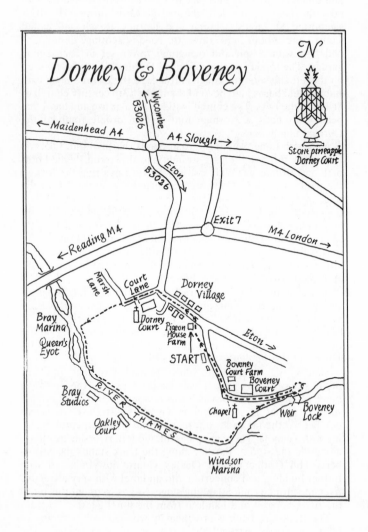

Dorney & Boveney

N

Stone pineapple
Dorney Court

and small. Go past the entrance to Dorney Court on the left and take the lane on the left about 100 yards further on. It is signposted St James' Church and Dorney Reach and called Court Lane. About $\frac{1}{4}$ mile down the road is a cottage of unknapped flint with a splendid octagonal tower set in a charming garden. The topiary in the garden of Dorney Court can be seen on the left and soon the coach entrance to the Court is seen with stabling and barns and, beyond them, the 13th century church of St James the Less. The church is still in regular use and has a fine peal of six bells, a Norman font and an ornate tomb of the Garrard family.

At Marsh Lane, where the road bends sharply right, take the farm track through the gate straight ahead marked Public Footpath and Bridleway. Walk south-westward ignoring the fork in the path on the left. Cultivated farmland lies on the left of the track and on the right side the lush meadows are bordered by a thick ancient hedge of mixed brush and trees. Alongside the path in summer flowers of pink mallow, blue chicory and bladder campion form bright patches of colour. The busy M4 motorway runs parallel with the track some $\frac{1}{2}$ mile away to the right and, lifting above the trees on the hill beyond, the bright green spire of Taplow parish church can be seen.

In a little over $\frac{1}{2}$ mile the track creeps through the hedge to emerge on the riverbank opposite the busy and colourful Bray Marina. Turn left and follow the towpath alongside the river. A heavily wooded island of mixed trees, Queen's Eyot, lies on the Berkshire side on the right. On the island is a small pavilion which can just be glimpsed through the dense foliage.

Shortly the ramshackle, down-at-heel buildings of Bray Studios appear on the opposite bank. This was the erstwhile home of Hammer Films which was famous for its horror movies such as Count Dracula, but much of the studio now seems derelict. At the far end is a rather curiously battlemented building with a cupola. There are pleasant, modern riverside dwellings alongside the studio. Further along the bank stands the Strawberry Hill Gothic pile of Oakley Court, now enlarged with further building and converted into an hotel with very attractive riverside grounds and a landing stage. Swans frequent this bit of the river, hopeful of a handout from the hotel guests.

The Berkshire bank is now heavily wooded with a variety of interesting trees, particularly a row of tall, slim poplars. The autumn colour of the leaves reflected in the water is truly magnificent. The Buckinghamshire bank, where the bed has been dredged out to deepen the river for boats, is steeply banked and overgrown with tall grasses and reeds. Here and there are tiny 'coves' where it is possible to climb down to the water or sit on the bank and admire the tranquil scene or watch the rivercraft glide by.

Soon the huge and unsightly spread of buildings of Windsor Marina come into sight, but alongside this is a carefully managed and well-screened caravan park which merges well into the river landscape. A large half-cylindrical boathouse with dozens of slender skiffs inside it is passed and here, just visible above the trees diagonally to the right, can be seen the Round Tower of Windsor Castle. Through a bit of scrub the towpath emerges onto the immaculate lawns and garden of Boveney Lock. On fine summer days the lock-keeper is kept busy all day as boats queue on either side for entry to the lock.

Immediately after the lock turn left onto a lane which doubles back parallel with and only a few yards from, the towpath. There are some fine examples of horse chestnut trees forming an avenue and arching over the lane. Continue along this lane and, ignoring the footpath on the right, go over the cattle grid and ahead passing the wrought-iron gates of Boveney Court on the right. Two rampant lions squat on top of the gateposts. The E-shaped house is a beautiful warm brick and timber 15th century dwelling of substantial size. It is now a private house but was once the property of the nearby Abbey of Burnham. Follow the lane past the house and then it is well worth bearing left along a small footpath to see the chapel of St Mary Magdalene, the chapel of ease for Boveney Court. There has, history states, been a place of worship on this site since before the Norman Conquest but the present chapel is of 12th and 13th century origin. It has chalk-rubble walls faced with flint and a weather-boarded bell-turret. The chapel was probably used by bargees and other rivermen when there was a busy wharf nearby used for loading and transporting timber from Windsor Forest. Now the chapel has a rather forlorn and lost air about it.

Retrace the path back to the lane and turn left on to it. Very soon it bears sharply right past Boveney Court Farm where there are some handsome and well-kept timber barns. Follow the lane across the flat meadowland where peewits may often be seen and, in summer, many swallows dip and swoop over the grass. To the right over the fields can be seen the chapel of Eton College and Windsor Castle. Passing some houses on the left, the last of which is called 'Wakemans', avoid the more major road ahead by striking off across the common on the left past the riding school, The Spanish Bit, and so back to Pigeon House Farm and the parked car.

Historical Notes:

Dorney Court lies at the end of the main street of the village, a beautifully preserved Tudor manor house. There has been a house on the site since before the Norman Conquest but the present building dates from 1510. It was bought by Sir James Palmer in 1600 and has remained in the family ever since. The Great Hall, where the Manor Court was held, contains portraits of twelve generations of Palmers by Lely, Kneller, Janssen and others. Sir James Palmer was Chancellor of the Garter to Charles I, his son, Phillip, was a colonel in the Royalist army and his second son, Roger, was married to the notorious Lady Barbara Palmer, Countess of Castlemaine, the King's mistress.

Today the family still farms the surrounding area, on a slight rise above the Thames flood plain. Even so, until recently, the land flooded regularly in winter time. A new breed of sheep has been developed here.

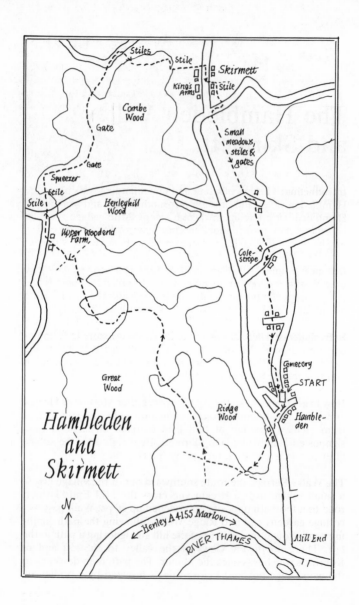

The Hambleden Valley and Skirmett

Introduction: This is a pleasant and undemanding walk along the Hambleden valley and through surrounding hills and woodlands. Hambleden itself is an attractive sleepy little village with an enormous church surrounded by charming cottages. Skirmett is a tiny hamlet of timber-framed, colour-washed and brick cottages.

Distance: 9 miles. Allow about 3½ to 4 hours for the walk to give time to stop and look at the marvellous countryside. There is one fairly abrupt climb near the middle of the walk; the rest is gentle ascent and descent. O.S. Map 175 Windsor and Reading.

Refreshments: There are two pubs and a village store in Hambleden and a pub, *The King's Arms*, in Skirmett at about the halfway mark. Bar food is served in the pubs and drinks, crisps and biscuits etc can be had at the village shop.

How to get there: Take the A4155 from either Marlow or Henley and, after about 6 miles from Marlow turn right or about 4 miles from Henley turn left at Mill End onto an unclassified road signposted Hambleden and Skirmett. Bear right into the village after one mile and park the car by the church.

The Walk: Retrace the route southward out of the village across a small bridge over a stream and cross the Mill End/Skirmett road to a footpath opposite approached up steps. Walk past two cottage gardens and into Ridge Wood following the path climbing gently round the contour of the hill and ignoring a path to the left. There are lovely views of the valley to the left and of Kenrick's which was once the Manor. The path then descends to the wood edge but, just before this, is bisected by a bridleway.

Turn right on to the bridleway and walk for about ¾ mile with excellent views of farmland to the left and a wooded hilltop to the right. The bridleway emerges onto a track into the Greenlands estate where turn right again and follow this track for some miles along the valley floor and ascending gently into Great Wood, a large area of colourful mixed woodland some of which has been newly planted with beech and conifer. Ignore all side paths and keep on the main track. Look out for white footpath arrows, also for large dark blue campanula flowers and purple wild mint, much haunted by butterflies. The walker may be fortunate enough to spot deer in the wood.

Turn left after about 2 miles at a grassy open space where there appears to be a grass 'ride' between the trees ahead and go on climbing gently out into open country. At a T-junction formed by a farm track turn left and at a Y-junction a few yards further on, bear right alongside Upper Woodend Farm to reach a lane at the farm entrance. Here turn right and walk up the lane for ⅓ mile to a T-junction. Cross the road and go over a stile on the opposite side; this is hidden behind a zigzag road bend sign. Go straight across the field from the stile to another stile into woodland and follow the well-defined path downhill to a track. Go through the 'squeezer' and turn right onto the track. After about 100 yards bear right onto a bridleway and follow this, through a gate, into a conifer plantation and then through another gate into less gloomy mixed woodland and so downhill into the valley for about a mile, disregarding diversions. The track finally emerges onto a minor road where turn right again. High on the hilltop to the left is a magnificently restored windmill.

In 200 yards go over a stile on the right into woods and follow the path past a North Sea Gas pipeline and across a field then over a stile into Combe Wood. Climb steeply up along a well-defined path with marvellous views of the lush valley below and bear left at a T-junction. Notice two trees which have grown so closely together that their trunks appear to be kissing. Go downhill and, at the wood edge, turn right and walk alongside the wood through a narrow path with a barbed wire fence on the left and then turn left at the field corner to walk downhill between the barbed wire on the left and a wooden fence on the right to Poynatt's Farm. Go over the stile onto a track and walk straight ahead to a road. Turn right and enter the hamlet of

Skirmett whose 19th century flint church has now been converted to a dwelling house. Just before reaching the *King's Arms* turn left onto a footpath and, after 100 yards, turn immediately right over a stile and follow an indeterminate path along the back of a bungalow and the field edge to a stile in the hedge at the far end. Go over the stile and turn right again into an old sunken lane. Just after a black and white cottage on the left, turn left onto a waymarked public footpath.

Walk due south now over the small lush meadows and several stiles. Cross a lane onto a path opposite going along the backs of cottages and their gardens and keep straight on along the track through the fields to emerge onto a lane at Little Colestrope, a splendid 17th century farmhouse with handsome barns and on down the lane to Colestrope Farm on the left. Cross the road and go through the gate onto the footpath and then through another gate keeping to the path above the field edge. Go over a stile and through two 'kissing' gates and alongside a garden to a driveway. Cross the drive and continue on a grassy path between more cottages and their colourful gardens and so into a grass field. Go through two gates and into another grass field. You will see Hambleden church just ahead. After about 30 yards take a stile in the hedge on the left and turn right onto the lane leading into the village. Notice the splendid cemetery gate, a memorial to the great W H Smith, the first Viscount Hambleden. On the left also are some well-built flint and brick cottages for the estate workers and soon Hambleden Manor comes into view. Turn right past the churchyard end, and back to where the walk began.

Historical Notes:

St Mary's Church, Hambleden, dates from the 11th century when it was a simple cruciform with a central tower but the north transept was extended in the 13th century. In 1703 the tower collapsed and was rebuilt in 1721 and, in 1883, was encased in flint and decorated with four little turrets each bearing a weather-vane. There was much restoration in 1859 when the 'sheepfold' for the farm labourers was transformed into a south Lady chapel. Among the yew trees in the churchyard is the domed 18th century mausoleum of the Kenrick family.

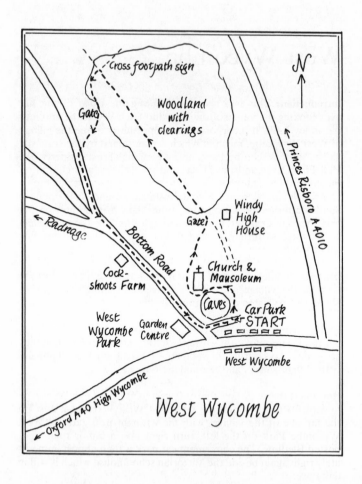

Cross footpath sign

Woodland
with
clearings

Gate

← Radnage

Bottom Road

Gate

Windy
High
House

← Princes Risboro A4010

Church &
Mausoleum

Cock-
shoots Farm

CAVES

Car Park
START

West
Wycombe
Park

Garden
Centre

West Wycombe

← Oxford A40 High Wycombe

West Wycombe

West Wycombe

Introduction: This is a short walk along the ridge of the hill over-looking the valley of the Wye and High Wycombe and into the valley itself. It incorporates an opportunity to see the village of West Wycombe, much of which is maintained by the National Trust, West Wycombe Park, also a National Trust property, the Hell Fire Caves and the Dashwood mausoleum and church on the hilltop. The church is famous for the golden ball which tops it and which can be seen for some distance around. It is open on Sunday afternoons and on some other days from 2 pm to 5 pm from April to October. On payment of a small fee the tower may be climbed, affording a magnificent view of the surrounding countryside.

Distance: 3 miles – an easy 1½ hours walk leaving time to browse through the village and visit the caves and church. O.S. Map Sheet 165 Aylesbury & Leighton Buzzard.

Refreshments: There are two pubs in the village both serving bar food. The cafe at the entrance to the caves is open when they are – most days during the summer – from 11 am to 5.30 pm and coffee, light snacks and tea may be bought there.

How to get there: Follow the A40 westward from High Wycombe toward Oxford through the village of West Wycombe. Just on the far side of the village, with the wrought-iron gates of West Wycombe Park on the left, turn right into a minor road sign-posted Bledlow. The convenient car park is then almost immediately right again beside the Victorian schoolhouse which is still in daily use.

The Walk: From the car park turn right and walk steeply uphill to the entrance to the caves which are well worth a visit. The man-made tunnel penetrates the hillside for $\frac{1}{2}$ a kilometre and the chambers have fanciful names such as Banqueting Hall, Monk's Cell and Inner Temple. Immoral and pagan meetings were reputed to take place in the caves and, nowadays, models provide a lifelike demonstration of these.

Having left the caves, take the steep, stepped path to the left up to the mausoleum, a large, open hexagon of flint with Portland stone dressing. On the way up, pause to look back eastward at the marvellous view of the road snaking back along the Wye valley and into High Wycombe. The three eastern sides of the mausoleum are in the shape of triumphal arches while the three on the west have niches to accommodate funerary urns. Keeping the mausoleum on the right, follow the path round to the front of the church of St Lawrence, set in the ditch and bank of an Iron Age fort.

Leaving the church, turn right along the gravelled path and through the churchyard gate. Follow the path diagonally across the grassy upland. To the left the landscape falls sharply away to a deep valley where small farms snuggle. Across the valley the hills rise steeply again and it is interesting to note the chalky white edges to the fields as the cultivated upland meets the woods on the hilltop. With luck, the walker may here observe a pair of sparrow-hawks planing in the thermals above the valley and hovering over prey in the scrubby grassland.

At the edge of the grassy plateau, where the path is joined by a narrow lane at Windy High House, bear left along a path leading into woodland through a wooden gate. Follow the path through the wood which gives way from time to time to afford wide views of the valley and hills on the right. Ignore tracks coming in on the left until a crossway is reached at the wood edge, with a cross footpath sign on a post. Turn sharply left and follow the path downhill quite steeply to a small wooden gate at the edge of the wood. Go through the gate and turn left. The path follows the contour of the slope across scrubby grassland and then down the edge of the field through a small jut of wood to emerge onto a lane. Orchids may be seen dotted about the scrub on the hillside where harebells grow. Along the field edge, tall yellow spikes of mullein jostle with feathery lady's bedstraw and scarlet pimpernel.

Follow the ancient sunken lane to the left between high hedges where flat plates of giant hogweed stand out. Soon the gilded ball of St Lawrence's church tower comes into sight lifting above the variegated trees on the hillcrest to the left, and bushes of hazel, nut-bearing in the autumn, fill the hedge. Turn left onto the unclassified road – Bottom Road – leading to Radnage past a row of houses.

Keep on along the lane, passing more houses on the left. On the right the warm red brick and tile of the barns of Cockshoots Farm peep from behind a thicket of trees. The farmyard is enclosed by a typical Bucks flint and brick wall. A little further along on the right the grounds of West Wycombe Park can be seen with the cricket field in the foreground.

At West Wycombe Garden Centre on the right, bear left and follow the rough path over the grass back to the car park or to look round the village and park.

Historical Notes:

West Wycombe: The village is dominated by the great hexagonal flint mausoleum and the church with its golden ball on the hilltop, 646 feet above sea level. Most of the village is in the hands of the National Trust and is of 16th and 18th century domestic architecture. In 1929 a large part of it was purchased by the Royal Society of Arts and the houses were repaired and modernised while still retaining the character of their earlier origin. The National Trust took over in 1934.

St Lawrence's Church: The church is medieval in origin and served the small settlements around its feet as well as the village of West Wycombe. It now has a Georgian nave provided, around 1765, by Sir Francis Dashwood, as were the stalls and lectern, in rosewood. The font has four doves round its bowl, threatened by a snake creeping up the slender clawed tripod. The gilded ball on top of the church was added in 1763, a copy of one on the Customs Building in Venice.

West Wycombe Park: The 18th century Italianate Palladian house, with temples and arches, a landscaped park and lake, church, caves and mausoleum, are all part of a landscape scheme started with classic splendour by Sir Francis Dashwood, 15th Baron Le Despencer. It is debatable whether Sir Francis and his friends actually practised Black Magic in the 'Hell Fire' caves after the disbanding of the notorious Hell Fire Club which met at Medmenham Abbey on the Thames near Marlow. Certainly the caves have a somewhat sinister air about them. Dashwood was leader of the Dilettante Society from its foundation in 1736 and celebrated architects such as Robert Adam and Nicholas Revett were employed to carry out his undertakings, painters being brought from Italy to decorate the work. The mausoleum was erected by Sir Francis in 1762 with money left to him by Bubb Doddington, Lord Melcombe. The urns in the niches were to contain the hearts of members of the Hell Fire Club.

The house of West Wycombe Park is the centre of the estate acquired by the Dashwood family in 1698. Sir Francis Dashwood (1708–1781) succeeded to his father's estate and fortune at the age of sixteen. A young man of great wealth, taste and energy, he promptly set about remodelling what was basically, a red brick Queen Anne house into an elegant mansion with Palladian elevations and extensive porticos. The Music Temple, on an island in the lake, was designed by Nicholas Revett and forms the centrepiece of views from the house and up the valley toward Church Hill. The house and grounds are open to the public daily from June to August on all days but Saturday from 2 pm to 6 pm.